ADVANCED

FOREX SUPPORT RESISTANCE

A practical guide to advanced support and
resistance, identifying best entry and exit point,
minor, and major support and resistance area and
how to effectively use them in trading

Abraham Robert. C

In order to say thank you for purchasing this book, I offer the below video course and more to you as a token of appreciation

Find the Link to the bonus video courses at the end of the book

TABLE OF CONTENT

CHAPTER 1

INTRODUCTION

The terms "support" and "resistance" are another crucial group in technical analysis. You should become familiar with this idea from the beginning of your trading career since it will be brought up frequently! The easiest way to explain Support and Resistance is as graphical depictions of the tensions that arise between supply and demand in every particular market.

As a result, when markets rise, there is often a greater demand, and when they fall, there is typically a greater supply, with supply and demand balancing their power at a support level.

Technical analysis is based on the concepts of support and resistance. Think about trends which are a sequence of increasing support levels or dropping resistance levels. or patterns on charts created by alternating between levels of support and resistance.

Alternatively, Fibonacci, which denotes figuring out which levels of resistance and support to utilize as a beginning point.

Even traders who primarily rely on indicators to guide their trading will highlight important support and resistance levels on the chart.

All too frequently, novice traders jump directly to indicators and systems in the hopes of discovering the holy grail setup that enchants them into lucrative trades, neglecting to have a thorough grasp of support and resistance analysis.

One of the most fundamental abilities that any price action trader has to possess is the ability to accurately sketch levels of support and resistance. It serves as the foundation for all subsequent methods, such as inside bars and pin bars in price action trading, and a suitable risk to reward ratio.

Trading starts to become easy if you get it correctly. If you make a mistake, trading will probably be a frustrating experience for you.

Ignoring support and resistance is a mistake since it is the most straightforward approach to comprehend the market and make trading decisions.

Recall that the price is the source of all indications. Support and resistance are not obtained from the price but from a human study of price activity.

A level known as support occurs when the price is mostly stopped from falling below it, whereas resistance

Resistance is where the price likely to be prevented from rising further through the level because the supply (sell side) is strong enough to retain the price at, or below, that level. It is a line drawn around the principal peaks. It is believed that there is sufficient demand (buy side) to support the price. It's a line drawn beneath significant level.

Pivot point levels, moving averages, or—most commonly just noting previous levels where the price struggled to break through can be used to determine Support and Resistance levels.

For a comprehensive understanding of all the basic of support and resistance, I suggest purchasing my book, Basic Forex Support and Resistance, from the Amazon store.

CHAPTER 2

MAJOR AND MINOR SUPPORT AND RESISTANCE AREA

Levels of minor resistance and assistance are insufficient. If the price is heading lower, for instance, it will reach a low, bounce, and then begin to decrease once more.

There is possible to designate that low as a minor support line or region because the price did stall out and then rebound from there.

However, given the downward trend, it is possible that the price will finally pass through that thin support line with little difficulty.

Little pockets of support or resistance might offer trading opportunities as well as analytical insights. In the previous example, we know the downtrend is still in place if the price does go below the minor support line. On the other hand, a range can be forming if the price stalls and then rebounds back at the previous low.

We have a higher low and a hint of a potential trend shift if the price pauses and rebounds above the previous low.

Important price levels that have lately prompted a trend reversal are known as major support and resistance lines or regions. The point at which the price reverted into a downtrend after it was going higher is a powerful resistance line. A strong support line is where a downtrend stops and an upswing starts.

The price will frequently find it difficult to break through a significant support or resistance line and resume its previous trajectory. For instance, the price will frequently rise after falling to a strong support line. Price retreats from the level several times before breaking through, however it may break through at some point.

Not every degree of resistance and support is the same. Major levels have the power to completely stop and reverse a trend, whereas minor levels will only momentarily halt rising or falling prices within a wider trend.

A market is perceived as stronger the more times it bounces off a support or resistance level. A significant resistance level may arise if the GBPJPY is unable to go over 1.2265, for example, reverting many times after reaching that level

A market may continue to move significantly in that direction if it breaks past a key level. We call this a breakthrough.

Major levels of support

For currency trading, major support levels are quite important. Using the price movement indication, skilled traders always execute their trades at the important support levels. Even while price action trading signals can be highly successful, you are under no obligation to employ them. It is also possible to build your trading strategy on the readings of basic indicators.

However, avoid overcomplication since this will provide you with an excessive amount of information and may force you to make a poor trading choice.

Minor support levels

For exact trade execution, minor support levels are also crucial. By employing the various time frame analysis in the Forex market, you may lower the amount of your stop loss. However, you must be aware of the danger involved in reduced time frame trading before you begin to trade it. By trading the lesser time frame, the majority of inexperienced traders lose a significant amount of money. You should use the lower time frame to assist you locate exact trade entries, but the higher time frame data should ultimately guide your trading decisions.

Resistance and support are very important

Why do resistance and support matter in trading?

Trade entries and exits

Entry and departure locations can be effectively guided by the use of resistance and support lines. A trader may decide to start a short position close to a resistance level or to launch a long trade close to a support level. Price breakouts or reversals are more likely to happen at certain points.

Identification of trends

Recognizing support and opposition facilitates trend identification. An asset's price may be considered to be in an upward trend if it regularly breaks above support levels.

When resistance levels are consistently tested and maintained, a downward trend may be verified. As a result, identifying these patterns is essential to making wise trading choices.

Indicators of volatility

When levels of support or resistance are crossed, it may indicate a shift in the mood of the market and more volatility. One may consider breakouts from these levels to be possible trading opportunities. This is primarily because they frequently generate notable price changes.

Psychological Importance

In the eyes of traders, support and resistance lines also have psychological significance. Buyers frequently consider an item to be a good chance to purchase when its price is getting close to a strong support level.

On the other hand, traders can consider resistance levels to be the best time to sell. Because traders' behavior based on these levels can influence price movements, this collective psychology can result in self-fulfilling prophesies.

Support and resistance levels are significant because they give traders essential knowledge about the status of the market right now and its possible course going forward. By putting stop-loss orders, these levels can assist traders in managing their risk and determining possible entry and exit opportunities for their trades.

Traders may also use support and resistance levels to recognize trends and trend reversals. Price movement beyond a resistance level in an asset might signal the start of a positive trend. The price of an asset may be a sign of a negative trend if it drops below a support level.

Furthermore, possible price objectives may be found by utilizing support and resistance levels. The price of an asset may climb further until it hits the subsequent resistance level if it breaks through one.

An asset's price may drop further until it hits the subsequent support level if it drops below one.

Place Stop-Loss Orders

In order to control their risk, traders can place stop-loss orders based on support and resistance levels. Traders may place a stop-loss order below the support level while initiating a long position. Traders may place a stop-loss order above the resistance level when initiating a short position.

Determine Trends and Trend Reversals

Traders may determine trends and trend reversals by using support and resistance levels. Price movement beyond a resistance level in an asset might signal the start of a positive trend. The price of an asset may be a sign of a negative trend if it drops below a support level.

Confirm Market signals

Traders can verify other market indications by utilizing resistance and support levels. A bullish trend may be confirmed, for instance, if the price of an asset breaks through a resistance level and a bullish candlestick pattern appears. It might be a sign of a negative trend confirmation if the price of an asset drops below a support level and a bearish candlestick pattern appears.

Determine Price objectives

Traders can determine possible price objectives by using support and resistance levels. The price of an asset may climb further until it hits the subsequent resistance level if it breaks through one. An asset's price may drop further until it hits the subsequent support level if it drops below one.

For traders attempting to negotiate the intricate world of financial markets, support and resistance lines are essential resources. These words offer priceless advice on managing risk, determining when to enter and exit the market, and gauging market emotion.

Keep in mind that trading has risks, therefore developing a comprehensive plan is crucial. To thrive in the markets, this has to take into account a number of things.

Trading using support and resistance levels necessitates a blend of technical analysis expertise and market understanding. To make wise trading selections, traders should thoroughly examine past price movements, the state of the market, and news and happenings in the market.

Risk Management

Determining the degrees of resistance and support can be helpful in risk management. In fact, to define risk and reward, stop-loss and take-profit orders are frequently placed close to these levels. Therefore, if a deal doesn't work out as expected, it's critical to know when to give up. Furthermore, where profits are taken matters when it comes to risk management and maintaining trading discipline.

Although levels of support and resistance can be useful tools in trading, it's crucial to keep in mind that there is always risk involved.

Before entering the market, traders have to have a well-defined risk management plan in place. This might entail employing suitable position sizing, placing stop-loss orders, and being fully aware of the possible risks and benefits of each trade.

Additionally, traders need to understand the limitations of resistance and support levels. Unexpected market developments may result in price moves that breach support and resistance levels, therefore these levels are not assured to hold.

Traders should constantly be ready for unforeseen changes in the market and modify their plans as necessary.

How to determine the level of Resistance and Support

Traders can determine levels of support and resistance using a variety of techniques. Finding price points where the asset's price has already reversed several times is the most popular strategy. These levels can happen at various times and might be sloping or horizontal.

Using technical indicators, such as trend lines, Fibonacci retracements, and moving averages, is another way to determine support and resistance levels.

Traders can use these indicators to pinpoint possible price points where an asset's price may reverse or consolidate.

Last but not least, traders may also employ chart patterns to pinpoint possible levels of support and resistance, such as head and shoulders, double tops and bottoms, and triangles. These trends might give important insights into the present and possible future direction of the market.

How to use support and resistance levels

Support and resistance levels may be used by traders in a variety of ways to increase trading profitability. We'll examine some of the most popular applications for these levels in trading.

A few crucial things to bear in mind in order to maximize the effectiveness of support and resistance level are as follows:

Multiple timeframes

To make support and resistance levels more dependable, confirm them across a range of timescales. On an hourly chart, a level of support that seems powerful on a daily chart might not be as important.

Dynamic character

Levels of resistance and support can change over time; they are not constant. To reflect changes in the dynamics of the market, traders should update their analysis on a frequent basis.

Verification

To verify the importance of support and resistance levels, utilize additional technical and fundamental analytical instruments. In this manner, you may avoid basing all of your trading decisions only on these lines.

Risk control

Principles of risk management should always be included in your trading plan. You avoid basing all of your hopes on a certain level of support or opposition as a result.

CHAPTER 3

HOW TO TRADE SUPPORT AND RESISSTANCE

Buying near support in uptrends, range segments, or chart patterns where prices are going upward, and selling/selling short near resistance in downtrends, range segments, or chart patterns where prices are moving downward, constitute the fundamental trading strategy using support and resistance.

Even when trading a range or chart pattern, it is beneficial to identify a longer-term trend. The direction to trade in is indicated by the trend.

For instance, if a range forms but the trend is still downward, it is preferable to short sell at range resistance as opposed to purchasing at range support.

The downward trend informs us that selling has a higher chance of yielding a profit than purchasing. If there is an upward trend and a triangle pattern appears, it is preferable to purchase close to the triangle pattern's support.

Although it can be profitable to buy close to support or sell close to resistance, neither of these levels of support nor resistance is guaranteed to hold. Thus, you might want to hold off until you have some assurance that the market continues to value that location.

If you plan to buy close to support, wait for a consolidation in that region before making the purchase when the price crosses over the upper bound of the little consolidation area. Such a rise in the price indicates that it is beginning to go higher off of support while also continuing to respect the support region.

When selling at resistance, the same idea holds true. When the price breaks below the tiny consolidation's low, you should begin a short trade. Watch for consolidation around the resistance region.

Put a stop loss few pips below the support level when buying, and several pip above the resistance level when shorting.

If you're holding out for a consolidation, when you purchase put your stop loss a few pips below the consolidation. The stop loss is placed a few pips above the consolidation while selling.

Have a target price in mind for a lucrative exit before you initiate a transaction. If you are buying near support, think about selling just before the price hits a level of significant resistance.

If you're shorting at resistance, get out before the market hits a significant level of support. At small resistance and support levels, you can also give up. Consider selling near the top of the channel, for instance, if you're buying at support in a rising trend channel.

Sometimes it makes more sense to wait for a breakout to happen rather than selling at slight resistance or support levels in order to maximize your profit. For instance, you could want to hold the trade until it breaks through triangle resistance and resumes the upswing if you're buying near triangle support inside a bigger rally.

Another idea is that previous support could give way to fresh opposition, or the other way around. While this isn't always the case, it does frequently function effectively in really certain situations, like a second chance breakout.

Because support and resistance are dynamic, so too must the trading choices you base them on. The most recent low and high are significant in an upward trend. A lower low in price suggests that there may be a shift in the trend; yet, a new high in price supports the upward trend. Pay close attention to the levels of support and resistance that are relevant at this moment.

Trends typically run into problems in their strong points. They could succeed in the end, but it usually takes time and several tries.

Make note of the key levels of support and resistance on your chart; if the price approaches those regions, they may become important once more. Once they are no longer relevant, delete them, as in the case where the price breaks through a strong resistance or support region and keeps moving well beyond it.

On your chart, note the minor support and resistance levels that are important and in effect right now. These will assist you in analyzing the ranges, chart patterns, and current trends. New minor support and resistance regions arise fast, making these minor levels obsolete. Continue sketching new regions of support and resistance, and cross out support and resistance lines that have been broken by the price.

If you are day trading, don't get too caught up in determining the support and resistance levels from previous days. Instead, concentrate on today. Information overload is readily caused by trying to look at too much data. Keep an eye on the current situation and take note of the degrees of support and resistance as they emerge.

It takes a lot of practice to trade off resistance and support. In a demo account, practice identifying trends, ranges, chart patterns, support, and resistance. Next, practice placing trades using objectives and stop-losses.

You should think about trading with real money only after you have been profitable with your support-and-resistance trading strategy for a few months.

Support And Resistance Trading Strategies

Trading in ranges or trading a consolidating market

With the goal of buying at the support line and selling at the resistance level, range trading takes place in the region between support and resistance lines. Keep in mind that resistance and support are not always represented by straight lines. Occasionally, noise will be present instead of a straight line. A trading range, or the zones of support and resistance, must be recognized by traders.

When the price bounces off the support line, traders are searching for long entry; when the price is close to the resistance level, they are searching for short entries.

Keep in mind that the asset's price may move outside of these ranges, so if you're going long, you should think about setting stop losses below support, and if you're going short, you should consider placing them above resistance.

Breakout trading

Often, the price breaks out and begins a new trend after a time of uncertainty. Traders often attempt to take advantage of these breaks above and below the resistance and support lines in order to benefit on any potential additional momentum in one direction.

When the price breaks out of its range, a breakout strategy seeks to enter the transaction. Strong momentum is what traders seek, and the breakout itself serves as a signal to enter a position and take advantage of the next market action.

Traders may place buy-stop and sell-stop orders, or they may take positions in the market, in which case they will need to actively watch the price movement. Usually, they will set the stop slightly above or below the previous support or resistance level. Traders can utilize traditional levels of support and resistance to determine their exit goals.

Using the breakout entry to enter a trade when the price breaks through a resistance level is one strategy. Many traders believe that the price has the momentum to move higher when it breaks through the barrier level.

The idea behind this is that traders who see a breach of resistance may be positive and will encourage the price to rise.

Many traders utilize this breakthrough from a resistance level as an entry point, albeit this may not always be the case.

Conversely, in the event that the price breaks through a support level, you might employ the breakout entry. A breach of support is typically interpreted as a warning that prices might decline much further. This breach of support is used by certain traders to profit from price declines.

You may utilize this entry approach for trading if you understand what support and resistance levels are and how to use them to determine when prices are breaking out of these levels.

You may use the Trading-View platform's charting feature to determine support and resistance levels whether you're using a real or demo trading account. Attempting to determine the support and resistance levels on various instruments at various times is also a very good idea.

It may be lot simpler for you to recognize any price breakouts after you are comfortable with and knowledgeable about these levels.

You should also keep in mind that, although trade entries are significant, they are only one aspect of your trading as a trader.

Having a good entrance plan is crucial. Nonetheless, having a rigorous risk management and exit strategy is as important. When used in tandem, entry, risk management, and exit strategy can assist you in developing into a knowledgeable trader.

False breakout trading

It is common for asset values to move a little bit farther than we anticipate. Although it doesn't occur frequently, when it does, it's referred to as a "false breakout." It is also feasible that the price may fall through $100, to $90.97 or $99.95, for example, and then begin to rise again if our research indicates that there is support at $100. Instead of a precise price, support and resistance are regions. Anticipate some volatility in the price's behavior in relation to support and resistance. It is improbable that it will end at the exact same cost as before.

False breakouts provide great possibilities for trading. One tactic is to hold off on entering the market until after a fake breakout has occurred. For instance, if the price is retreating to support and the trend is upward, wait for the price to break below it before buying when it begins to rise above it again.

In the same way, if the price is trending down and is retreating to resistance, wait for a price break over it before initiating a short sale when it begins to fall below it.

The drawback of this strategy is that a false breakout is not guaranteed. Good trading chances might be lost if you wait for one. It is therefore usually advisable to seize trade opportunities when they arise. It's a plus if you manage to spot the occasional false breakthrough trade.

Since false breakouts can happen sometimes, it is advisable to position your stop-loss somewhat away from resistance or support to reduce the likelihood that the false breakout will strike your stop-loss position before continuing in the direction you had planned.

Trendline trading

Using a trendline as support or resistance is recommended by the trendline trading method. Traders just link many highs or lows in an uptrend or downtrend by drawing a line. The price would move in the direction of the trend and rebound off the trendline if the trend was strong. In this instance, traders identify trend-following entry points.

"Trendlines," which are angled or horizontal lines, are used to indicate areas of support and resistance. A horizontal line is created to indicate that the market is having difficulty moving past a certain price area if the price stops and reverses in that same area twice in quick succession.

The price reaches greater highs and lower lows during an uptrend. The price reaches lower highs and lower lows during a downturn. Join the peaks and troughs of a trend. Then, to assess where the price could eventually encounter support or resistance, extend that line to the right.

These straightforward lines draw attention to ranges, trends, and other chart patterns. They provide traders an idea of the direction the market is now taking as well as potential future directions.

CHAPTER 4

ENTRY

The price or level at which a trader initiates a trade (buy/sell) in forex is known as the entry point. Because there are so many different factors that may influence the forex market, traders may find it difficult to choose a forex entry point.

Finding an entrance confirmation for trade entry at the optimal trade entry point is necessary once we have determined the market trend and are prepared to initiate a trade in a possible trade region.

We will avoid making haphazard trades if we have the ideal trade entrance approach. It discovers timely, high-quality forex trades with reliable entry signals that behave as we would anticipate in our possible trading region.

Each and every forex trader has a profitable trading approach. It might be a trading strategy based on supply and demand, price action, Elliott wave, or another approach. Most merchants have no trouble locating possible trading regions. However, the majority of them lack ideal entrance tactics to find acceptable entry points

They deal heedlessly. It's the same strategy as not looking both ways before crossing the street. Despite having successful trading methods, they lack the knowledge necessary to identify when to enter and quit the currency market.

The market execution price for the currency pair you are trading is defined at that time. The entry point will specify when the trade will begin.

In order to benefit at the end, the entry point for a currency pair purchase should be below the profit level.

To ensure that you finish up with a profit on a sell order, the entry point should be above the profit level.

The price at which you will enter the transaction was referred to as the entry point. The market should move in your favor when you initiate the transaction since that moment should be at its ideal location.

The right entrance point is difficult to forecast. If you trade, you are aware that the majority of your first entry result in losing trades.

That's what happens when you start trading and the market moves against you right away. The market chooses to reverse course rather than go in the way you had anticipated.

You need a strategy to assist you determine your entry point in order to make a successful entrance in the Forex market.

You shouldn't have too many issues if you have a solid plan in place and are waiting patiently for the entrance opportunity.

Your whole trading strategy may be strengthened and elevated with an effective entrance confirmation approach or entry technique. It is essential for effective forex trading management.

Entry Strategies

Candlestick Formation

Almost all traders choose this entry strategy since it is the most popular and trustworthy. Here, seasoned traders often employ patterns like the engulfing and shooting star.

Candlestick patterns pinpoint the precise entrance point at which the asset's price movement may begin to foretell its future direction. It increases the likelihood of success for the traders.

Chart Patterns

One of the most common trade entry strategies used by traders is the use of chart patterns as entry signals. In order to weather any significant price fluctuations, it helps us identify their source before they occur.

Despite being a stand-alone trading approach, the trading chart pattern may also be an excellent entrance method.

Some popular chart patterns are

- Head and shoulders
- Double top
- Double bottom
- Rounding bottom
- Cup and handle
- Wedges
- Pennant or flags
- Ascending triangle
- Descending triangle
- Symmetrical triangle

Breakouts Entry Point

Using breakouts as entry signals is one of the most often used trade entry tactics by traders. Finding important levels and taking advantage of them as trade entry points is known as breakout trading. Effective breakout methods require an understanding of price movement. The key component of breakout trading is when forex prices breach a predetermined level of support or resistance.

New traders should employ breakout entry points because this approach is so simple to apply.

One of the most common trade entry strategies for every trader is to use breakouts as indications. Classifying important levels and using them as indications to enter trades is known as breakout trading. When it comes to using breakout methods successfully, price action specialists are in the lead.

Trendlines Entry Point

Every fad has its backlash. At that point, the trend pauses, bounces back, and then keeps moving farther in the initial direction.

When the trend pauses and there is a retreat, it would be your entry point.

You can see the entry point much more clearly if you create horizontal resistance and support lines beside the uptrend or downtrend support and resistance line.

Different Time Frame

Over time, you will discover that you may choose the ideal entrance point by utilizing various time periods.

You should choose H4 or a daily time period if you want to follow the trend.

If you trade the H4 and daily time frames, you will reduce the amount of losing trades because those two time frames perform considerably better at following the trend.

You should pay attention to look at the H1 time frame after determining that the H4 or daily time frame is an appropriate time frame to trade.

For a longer time frame, the H1 time frame might provide you with a good entrance point around the support or resistance.

You reduce the likelihood of entering the trade too early or too late if you employ this type of technique.

One of the biggest issues faced by both novice and seasoned traders is the entrance point.

It is much easier if you know when to enter other items, but that is not always the case. Finding entry points might be challenging, so you'll need to practice defining them.

You can be certain that your ability to define entrance points will increase with time and experience.

CHAPTER 5

EXIT POINT

The price at which a trader closes a transaction in order to limit their losses or take a profit is known as the exit point. Selecting the ideal exit strategy aims to minimize losses and maximize gains.

Guidelines for choosing an ideal forex trading exit point.

Take Profit Orders

When a certain profit threshold is met, a trade is automatically closed using take profit orders. By using this strategy, traders may lock in profits and reduce the chance that they will be lost as a result of an unexpected price reversal.

Take-profit orders have to be placed in accordance with the trader's trading plan and risk tolerance.

A take-profit order, for instance, may be placed by a cautious trader 10% above the entry price or, more aggressively, 20% or more above the entry price.

Stop Loss Orders

When a certain loss threshold is met, a trade is automatically closed using stop loss orders. By using this strategy, traders may control their losses and lower their chance of losing more than they can afford to lose.

Stop loss orders have to be placed in accordance with the trader's trading strategy and risk tolerance.

A cautious trader would place a stop loss order at a price that is 5% below the entry price, whereas an aggressive trader might place one that is 10% or more below the entry price.

Trailing Stop Loss Orders

When the price swings against the transaction, trailing stop loss orders are utilized to automatically cancel a position. With this strategy, traders may lock in profits and hold onto the transaction in the event that the price moves further in their favor.

A trader's trading strategy and risk tolerance should be taken into consideration when setting trailing stop loss orders. An aggressive trader would place a trailing stop loss order at a price that is 10% or more below the current price, whereas a prudent trader might place one at a price that is 5% below the current price.

Fundamental Exit

Based on news and market factors, you can close a position. For instance, you may decide to leave a position after bad news or close out of your short-term investments before a significant news announcement.

Risk/Reward Stop

When using a risk/reward stop, you modify your stop loss so that there is always a minimum risk/reward ratio of 1:1. If your trade approaches, but does not reach, your profit objective, then reverses, this effective strategy lets you keep your earnings.

Account Target

You may terminate all of your positions in your account after you reach a particular account-based goal, such 25% for the month.

Scale-Out

Scaling out means leaving parts of your position according to several standards.

To catch the major winnings, you could, for instance, take a tiny amount off when the market initially makes some accessible, some more at a pre-planned objective, and some more on a following stop.

An exit point is the price at which a trader or investor has to liquidate their stake. Typically, an investor would purchase long-term assets while selling to exit their investment. When a trader is short, they might purchase to cover the gap, or they can sell at an exit point.

Depending on a trader's or investor's plan, the exit point can be determined in advance. Alternatively, the departure point might be established based on current market circumstances or other life variables, such selling off other assets to cover a payment.

Frequently, an order is given to trigger the exit after an exit location has been created. A profit or loss may be realized at the departure point, depending on how the price changed after the purchase.

Exit points can be used to define benefit objectives and control the risk of failure. Investors usually utilize conditional instructions to indicate when they want to get out.

One exit method that includes planned departure points during the first investing period is a bracketed buy order. A purchase order with brackets is a conditional order that has an exit stop loss point and a profit goal. An investor buys a safe using a bracketed purchase order, and then locks in a profit by setting a profit target order at a particular price.

In the unlikely event that the price goes against the investor's expectation, the stop loss will be placed at a predetermined price to reduce risk. The location is now closed, so if one of the orders is executed, the other is cancelled. Depending on their investment objectives and risk tolerance, the investor may change the price of the stop-loss and benefit goal orders.

Why is having an exit strategy in trading necessary?

Whether you are trading forex, indices, or crypto currencies, developing a profitable trading system that works for you requires having an exit strategy.

Traders can choose from a wide variety of exits, some straightforward and some more intricate. The diversity of exits that are necessary to exchange what's in front of you and accomplish your goals adds to the complexity.

To ensure that you stick to your established trading plan, you must have an exit trading strategy in place. The objectives you are attempting to accomplish may suffer if you deviate from your plan and begin allowing your feelings to control your trading positions.

An exit strategy is a valuable addition to your overall trading plan as it guarantees that you apply appropriate risk and trade management strategies, which will increase your profitability as a trader.

In forex trading, choosing the appropriate entry and exit positions is crucial. To find possible entry and exit locations, traders might employ take profit orders, stop loss orders, trailing stop loss orders, technical and fundamental research, and news events. It's crucial to remember that forex trading entails risk, and one should never take on more risk than one can afford to lose.

Before selecting your exit strategy, there are a few elements to take into account

- Risk-Reward ratio
- Bid/Ask spread
- Risk tolerance
- Trading style

Risk-Reward Ratio

What is the objective? To what extent do you wish to earn? To what extent are you prepared to lose? In this deal, how much risk can you afford to take? These kinds of inquiries will aid in ascertaining the optimal exit trading technique for any unique circumstance.

Bid/Ask Spread

In order to settle their trades at a desirable price while exiting a position, traders frequently require liquidity from other market players who have not yet closed their holdings. We can gauge how long it will take these new players with open positions (the "bids") to fill our orders (the "asks") by using the bid/ask spread.

The gap between the ask and bid prices for a particular security is known as the bid-ask spread. The ask price is the lowest amount a seller is ready to take, and the bid price is the maximum amount a buyer is willing to pay for the security.

Who sets the asking and bid prices?

All parties involved in the market determine prices. Consider every possible trader you may come across: financial counsellors, retail investors just like you, and investors from large institutions (think hedge funds, banks, pension funds, mutual fund managers, etc.).

Since several individuals and organizations are interested in trading lots of varying sizes, a mechanism for facilitating these deals must exist. The main responsibility of a market maker is to connect vendors and customers.

Market makers contribute significantly to the financial markets' liquidity, or the ease and speed with which purchases and sales may be made. Buying and selling at the time and price you desire would be far more difficult without market makers to mediate deals.

Risk Tolerance

A high-risk tolerance indicates a willingness to take on greater risks and absorb greater losses in the hopes of maybe increasing gains.

If necessary, you can employ the stop-loss exit trading method in this situation, extending the stop-loss distance from your entrance price point. The amount of money at risk each time something may go wrong is reduced if you have a low risk tolerance. For traders who are uncomfortable taking significant risks, this might help ease their minds.

All exit trading methods are based on the idea of risk management, which helps us choose when it's time to stop losing money or lock in profits before they become unachievable (or just too hazardous).

Style of Trading

It's crucial to take your trading style into account when selecting your exit plan.

While some traders may be more willing to take on bigger losses in order to avoid losing out on even bigger rewards down the road, others may want to reduce risks and lock in gains as soon as feasible.

If you're conservative about your trades but want greater control over timing them so that they happen at places where there's still time to make up some ground, then utilize the stop-loss exit trading method with a longer distance from the entrance price point, if needed.

You may manage your position based on market developments after you enter by keeping a range of exit strategies in your toolkit. Then, to maximize the outcome of your deal, you may keep a careful eye on the market and adjust as needed.

As a trader, all you can do is plan and then execute. Once you complete the deal you are merely experiencing, not producing. Rather than making your exit based on a flawless replication of a historical pattern that matches your back-tested indicators, you should base it on what the market is doing at the moment.

It's not hard to do, particularly if you enter simply and use the appropriate exit in the appropriate situation.

For optimum impact, we would always advise you to incorporate this lesson into your forex trading strategy and to step away from your trading plan or trading notebook. Choose one or two exits to practice with today from the list that you would want to add. You may return for more at a later time.

Combining Resistance and Support Levels In A Vertical And Horizontal Manner

Combining horizontal and vertical support and resistance levels can help traders improve their research and provide a more complete picture of the market.

The following are some advantages of combining these two forms of resistance and support:

Confirmation of key levels

Based on past price movement, such as swing highs and lows, vertical support and resistance levels are constructed.

Conversely, horizontal support and resistance levels are set at certain price points that have traditionally served as barriers. The combination of these two levels allows traders to confirm the importance of important price zones.

The correlation between vertical and horizontal levels enhances the dependability of the former and raises the possibility of price oscillations or reversals.

Confluence of signals

Strong trading signals can be obtained from the confluence of horizontal and vertical support and resistance levels. Converging levels indicate a greater likelihood of price movements. For instance, the resistance zone is strengthened and a possible short trading opportunity is indicated if a horizontal resistance level coincides with a falling trend line, which is a type of vertical resistance.

Enhanced Risk Management:

Traders may set more accurate stop-loss and take-profit levels by combining horizontal and vertical support and resistance levels. Traders can safeguard themselves from fictitious breakouts or breakdowns by positioning stop-loss orders just above both kinds of levels. In a similar vein, traders can benefit before prices possibly revert by placing take-profit orders close to the intersection of these levels.

Analysis of market structure

While horizontal levels provide a more accurate point of reference, vertical support and resistance levels shed light on price movements and market structure. Through an examination of the way price interacts with both kinds of levels, traders may learn more about the general mood of the market and spot possible turning points.

Adjusting entry and exit points

Traders have the chance to adjust their entry and exit points when vertical and horizontal levels coincide. An ascending trend line, which is a type of vertical support, and a horizontal support level, for example, may indicate a possible purchasing opportunity. This convergence can help traders enter deals more precisely and confidently.

Your research will be more robust when it includes both vertical and horizontal support and resistance levels.

This is because it helps you discover important price zones, validate signals, manage risk, examine market structure, and optimize entry and exit locations. Traders may boost their chances of success in the forex market and make better selections by combining these two sorts of levels.

CHAPTER 6

APPLYING SUPPORT AND RESISTANCE IN DIFFERENT MARKET CONDITIONS

Using resistance and support in various market circumstances

It is crucial to apply resistance and support in various market circumstances in order to adjust to shifting market dynamics. The following factors should be taken into account when using support and resistance levels in different market scenarios:

Applying support and resistance in a Trending Markets condition

✓ When the market is in an uptrend, watch for chances to purchase when it retraces around support levels. There may be opportunities to join the rising trend at these support levels.

✓ When the market is in a downward trend, watch for chances to sell when it approaches resistance levels. These resistance levels may be useful as possible places of entry for taking advantage of the downward trend.

Applying support and resistance in a ranging market condition

✓ Determine the important price levels that fall and rise within a range. Seek for opportunities to sell near resistance and purchase near support. Until a breakthrough happens, traders can try to make money on price fluctuations that stay inside the defined range.

Applying support and resistance in a break out markets

- ✓ Keep a careful eye on levels of support and resistance for any possible breakouts. A significant move in price above or below support or resistance signals a change in the mood of the market and is referred to as a breakout.
- ✓ When a breakout happens, traders may think about making an entry in that direction with the goal of taking advantage of a significant price move.

Applying support and resistance in a Consolidating market

- ✓ Pay attention to the shorter-term support and resistance levels inside the consolidation pattern during periods of consolidation, when the price is range-bound and its swings are getting smaller.

✓ Traders might search for opportunities to purchase the consolidation pattern around its lower boundary (support) and sell it near its higher limit (resistance).

Applying support and resistance in a reversal markets

✓ When the price gets close to important levels of support or resistance, keep an eye out for any reversals. These pricing points may serve as pivotal points where the price changes course.

✓ To support the argument for a reversal, look for further confirmation indications such candlestick patterns, trend line breaks, or technical indicators.

✓

Recall that market circumstances are subject to change, therefore it's critical to evaluate the entire picture before assigning support and resistance levels. To improve your analysis, take into account variables like news stories, market volatility, and the general trend.

Furthermore, in order to find support and resistance levels that match over several time horizons and thus increase their relevance, it is essential to employ numerous time frames.

You may improve your chances of success in the forex market by making better educated trading selections by adjusting your approach to resistance and support based on the current state of the market.

Confluence in trading

We must first define confluence before delving into the specifics of how it might enhance your trade. The definition given by the dictionary is as follows.

Confluence: a circumstance in which two events coincide or come together.

Confluence, then, is simply the result of two or more "things" coming together simultaneously. Confluence is the result of two or more components coming together at the same location on a chart, as it relates to Forex trading.

These "things" might include something as basic as a strong trend, a moving average, a buy or sell signal in price movement, or even a critical support or resistance level. Confluence factors are the sum of all of these elements. Put differently, one element may be a strong trend, another could be a buy signal from price action, and so on.

Confluence trading is a potent strategy used in forex that combines many indicators or tools for technical analysis to find high-probability trading opportunities.

Several main justifications for the significance of confluence trading

Enhanced trading Confidence

Traders' confidence in their ability to make decisions is bolstered when a number of indicators or analytical methods line up and produce the same signal. Confluence serves as a confirmation mechanism that raises the possibility of a successful transaction while decreasing the possibility of misleading signals.

Greater Probability Setups

Confluence trading gives traders the opportunity to pinpoint setups that have a better chance of succeeding. Trader quality may be reduced by focusing on trades that are more likely to result in a profit by needing numerous criteria to align, such as trend lines, support and resistance levels, chart patterns, or technical indicators.

Enhance Proper risk management

Confluence trading can help traders better control their exposure to risk. Traders can determine critical levels for stop-loss placement or profit goals by combining several techniques. Effective risk management requires the ability to create suitable risk-reward ratios and identify the best times to enter and exit trades. These skills are provided by this method.

Confluence trading encourages traders to make decisions with greater objectivity

Traders take into account a variety of criteria while making trading decisions, as opposed to depending only on one indication or analysis method. This promotes more disciplined and reliable trading techniques by lowering emotional biases and impulsive trading.

Ability to Adjust to Market Conditions

Markets are ever-evolving and subject to quick changes. Confluence trading gives traders the flexibility to use a range of indicators or analytical tools to adjust to shifting market circumstances. Because of this flexibility, traders may better take advantage of a variety of trading opportunities by modifying their methods in response to changes in the market, the strength of a trend, or other pertinent variables.

Price Action Confirmation

Confluence trading demonstrates how important price action is. Trading professionals are able to verify and authenticate the indications produced by price fluctuations by combining several indicators or tools.

This strengthens the idea that price action is a major market driver and that having numerous indications pointing in the same direction strengthens the foundation for making decisions.

In conclusion, confluence trading is beneficial in the forex market because it boosts traders' confidence, raises the likelihood of profitable trades, helps with risk management, encourages unbiased decision-making, adjusts to market circumstances, and validates price movement. In the volatile forex market, traders can enhance their trading tactics and get superior outcomes by pursuing confluence in technical analysis.

Managing Emotions When Trading

If you wish to avoid allowing bad feelings to influence your trade, you must carefully consider your strategy. In the financial markets, the proverb "Failing to plan is planning to fail" might really come to pass.

There are several ways to turn a profit as a trader. There are several tactics and methods available to traders to assist them in reaching their objectives. However, whatever strategy is going to be effective for that individual will typically be defined and methodical as opposed to being based solely on "hunches."

Strategies to help you feel more in charge of your feelings when trading

Establish Personal Guidelines

You can better manage your emotions when you establish your own guidelines for trading. Setting risk/reward tolerance thresholds for entering and leaving trades, through profit goals and/or stop losses, may be part of your rules.

Trade in Appropriate Market Conditions

It's wise to avoid unfavorable market situations as well. It's wise to refrain from trading when you're not "feeling it." If you aren't comfortable trading, the best course of action could be to simply walk away rather than depending on the market to lift your spirits.

Reduce the Size of Your Trade

Reducing the amount of your trades is one of the simplest methods to lessen their emotional impact.

Create a trading schedule and trading log

Regarding the fundamentals, one tactic to keep in mind before major news occurrences is to prepare for many scenarios.

There may be a significant difference in outcomes between novice traders who follow a strategy and those who don't. The first step in combating trading emotions is to draft a trading plan, but regrettably, this won't totally eliminate the impact of these feelings. It could be beneficial to keep a log of your forex trades.

Learn to relax while trading

You'll be more able to react sensibly in any market scenario if you're at ease and enjoy trading.